ARAM KHACHATURIAN

WALTZ
FROM "MASQUERADE"

Piano, Four Hands

Anglo-Soviet Music Press, London
Sole Selling Agents:
Boosey & Hawkes, Music Publishers Ltd.
for Great Britain and British Commonwealth of Nations (except Canada)

Le Chant du Monde, Paris
pour la France, Belgique, Luxembourg et les Pays francophones de l'Afrique

Japan-Soviet Music Inc., Tokyo
for Japan

G. Ricordi & C., Milano
per l'Italia

Musikverlag Hans Sikorski, Hamburg
*für die Bundesrepublik Deutschland einschl. West-Berlin, Griechenland, Israel,
Niederlande, Portugal, Schweiz, alle skandinavischen Länder (ohne Finnland),
Spanien und Türkei*

Edition Fazer, Helsinki
for Finland

ISBN 978-07935-3780-8

G. SCHIRMER, *Inc.*

DISTRIBUTED BY

HAL•LEONARD®
CORPORATION
7777 W. BLUEMOUND RD. P.O. BOX 13819 MILWAUKEE, WI 53213

for USA, Canada, Mexico, Central and South America

WALTZ
from "Masquerade"
for Piano, Four Hands

Transcription by A. Kondratiev

Aram Khachaturian

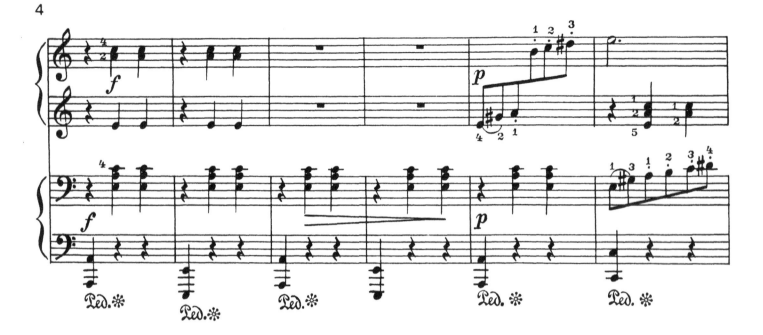

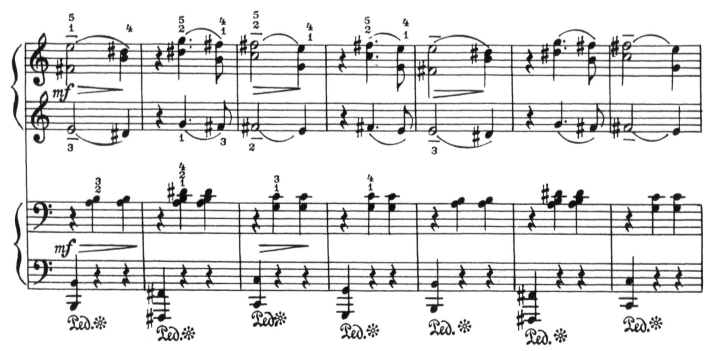

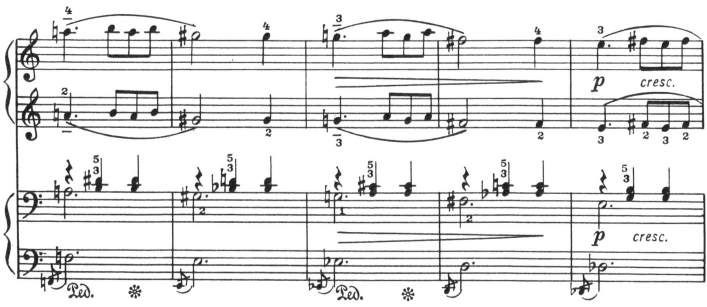

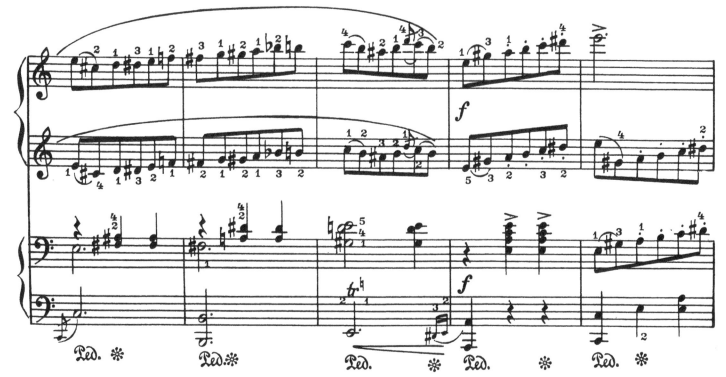

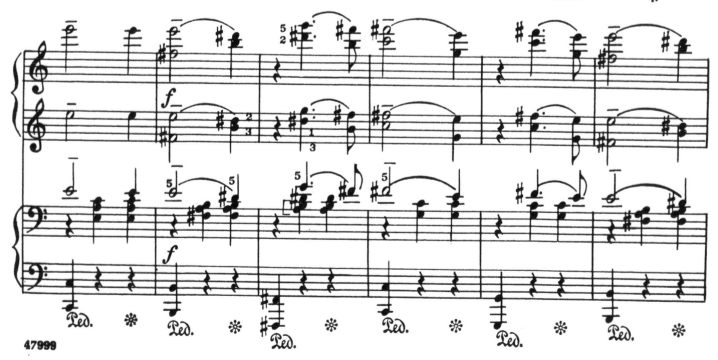

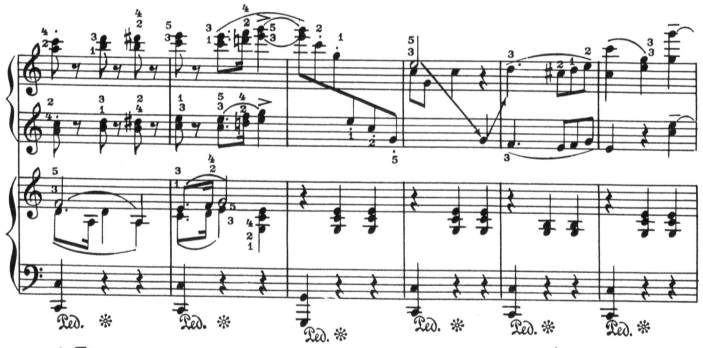

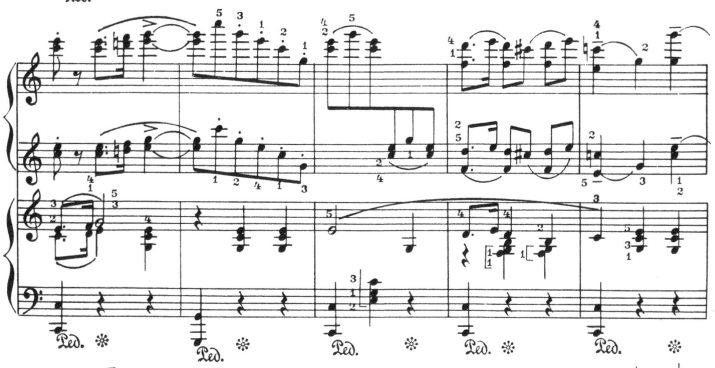

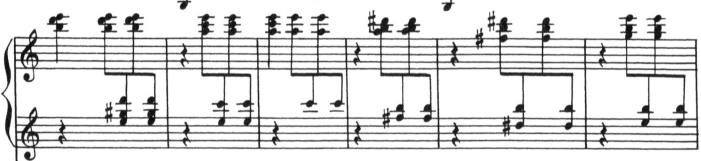

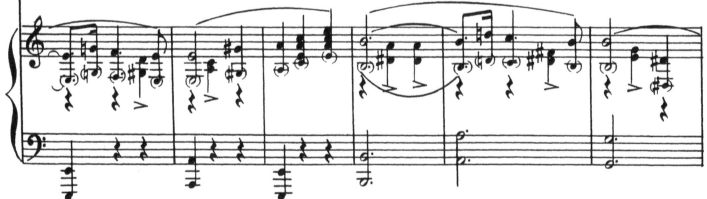

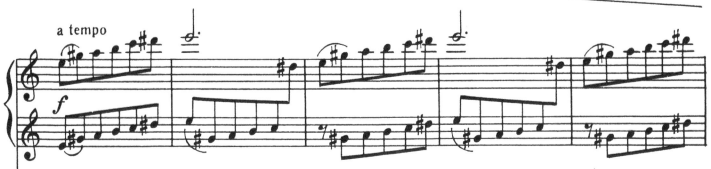

poco rit.

poco rit.

Ped. ✱